The Greatest

Debbie Allen's Hot Chocolate Nutcracker

Audition Story EVER!

By Tatiana Williams

Illustrated by Marieka Heinlen

ISBN: 1727253671

ISBN-13: 978-1727253672

Instagram: tatianaw85

Dedicated to HRW – Remember girls never give up.

Thank you, mom, Akina, Alex, Daniele and Fan.

Fame first came on TV in 1982. I was 11-years-old at the time and immediately hooked. I loved the show's premise, a group of kids finding their way through the Performing Arts school in New York City. And I loved all of its characters -- LeRoy, Coco, Danny, Bruno, and their teacher, Lydia Grant aka The Debbie Allen. "You want fame." She said in the opening credits. "Well fame costs and right here is where you start paying, in sweat." I was done. My narrow 11-year-old behind was about to sweat. I loved and still love everything about the woman.

Fast forward to the fall of 2015, I was now 43-years-old when I got the chance to audition for Debbie Allen. That's right, The Debbie Allen was about to hold auditions for her ballet and she was going to see <u>me</u> sweat.

For years Debbie Allen choreographed and produced *The Hot Chocolate Nutcracker*, a beautiful, multicultural ballet with talented dancers in all shapes and shades. The show is high energy, with vibrant colors and characters, from the sugar plum fairies with their light and airy toes to the candy cane boys and their heart-pounding hip hop moves, the show is a nonstop theatrical event! (Plug - you should get tickets when she does it again this winter.)

Debbie Allen wanted to audition roller skaters for one of the scenes in the ballet. I initially got the email because when she opened the Debbie Allen Dance Academy (aka DADA) in my neighborhood I went there hoping to bump into her.

Instead I got information about the emailing list and joined it so I could stay in the know with all things DADA-related, (well Debbie-related actually). My friend Lynne asked me about the audition since she got the email too. It pushed me to take a closer look. 32 years later could my *Fame* dream finally come true?

When I reread the information sent I immediately thought, "I could totally do this!" Yes I did. After emailing a few times with the coordinator to find out how much time I would need to devote to practice after getting the part (I do have a day job, you know), I decided to try out.

Now, at the time I didn't own a pair of roller skates but I still thought I could do this. I had skated for years and I could spin in a circle and even skate backwards.

Audition day arrived. Saturday morning, my original plan was to get my skates early and break them in but then mommy, wifey and lifey happened and oops I have NOOOOO skates. No matter, I had a date with destiny and The Debbie Allen and I won't let us down.

I drove to Big 5 Sporting Goods right before my audition, tried on a pair of roller skates, bought them and jumped in the car and went on my way. I didn't really think Debbie Allen would be there but still just knowing I was occupying the same space was enough for me.

When I got to DADA, racing to get inside the door, the other skaters had already gone inside the dance room to start the audition. Was I too late? Would they try to stop the dream? Please let me in, I have an audition to nail. At that point I started to have a bit of doubt. What if it was too hard for me? What if my basic skating skills weren't enough?

The nice girl at the front desk broke into my thoughts... "Here fill out this form, and take this number, hurry they just went in there!" She gave me the paperwork to hastily fill out along with an audition number to safety pin to my shirt. It was all so exciting. I felt so official, like I was on a real episode of "*Fame*!"

I had my skates in my arms and ran to the audition door. As I opened it a person on the other side pulled the door and said, "Good morning!" It was The Debbie Allen. It seemed as if a ray of light shined from her face onto mine! I almost fell then and there. I looked up at her beautiful smile and said to myself "Girl, you are not leaving this audition until they pull you out, <u>no matter what</u>."

The room had hardwood floors, two walls had floor to ceiling mirrors and dance bars on the non-mirrored walls. I officially felt official. There were about 10 girls all in their tweens wearing full-on dance gear. They had the leotards, the buns, the nude stockings with matching nude roller skates. I on the other-hand had on black leggings, cut-off jean short shorts, and a flash-dance t-shirt with my audition number neatly pinned to the front.

The beginning was easy enough. The choreographer (a guy in black skates with beautiful brunette hair, think John Travolta's hair in its prime) told all of us girls to skate in a circle. Sure thing boss, anything for you and Debbie. Now skate the other way? Okay, not a problem. Skate backwards. Done. Now skate backwards the other way. Easy peasy.

Then he told us to squat down and skate in a circle. What? That is when "no matter what" started to happen. I could barely squat all the way down. My shorts were cutting off the circulation into my upper thighs. I could barely feel my legs much less move them.

I tried and probably looked more like a sick baby duckling than a graceful swan. Then he asked us to squat, stick out one leg and skate in a circle. Is it getting hot in here? I quickly was lapped by the other skaters, who moved so fast and free. I was way out of my league. Oh snap, now what?

I continued to try and camouflage my less than perfect skating skills until the dreaded breakdown. The breakdown is where they have only a few skaters at a time audition in front of Debbie and the choreographer. Try as I might to look professional and limber, I saw them talking in mouth covered whispers and looking at me. I darted my eyes away, I knew my time had come. Shortly after the breakdowns The Debbie Allen called my name from her lips and beckoned me to her side, "Tatiana?"

I skate over slowly, super sweaty and super in awe. She smiled warmly, and I took this a cue to open my big mouth, "They're better than me, they're younger than me, I know." To which she sweetly replied, "It has nothing to do with age dear, nothing to do with age." Then I said, "They're just better." She answered as she shook her fierce head slowly, "This isn't for you, dear." Sad, I know.

But if she only knew, this was for me! I got to spend an hour with one of the people who had inspired me the most in my life. I got to sweat with The Debbie Allen. I conceded and thanked her. Then I asked her if we could take a picture together when she was finished with the audition. She gave me a sweet side-eye look only she could give and agreed. Yes!

As I exited, two angelic dancers came skate-floating in. They had on blue and red sequined skate dresses, skin-toned tights and matching skin-toned skates on their little legs, perfect buns on top of their perfect heads and pretty make-up. They looked so adorable, like jewelry-box ornaments that twirl when you wind them. I thought Debbie might have called for reinforcements.

After the audition I got my picture with Debbie and a lifetime of joy in the retelling of this story! The family and I went to *The Hot Chocolate Nutcracker* when it opened around Christmas. While I was amazed by all of it, I clapped extra loudly when the roller skaters took the stage.

THE END...

Made in the USA
Las Vegas, NV
14 December 2024

14283813R00015